W9-AGJ-660

WITHDRAWN

PROTECTING EARTH'S
LAND

VALERIE RAPP

PORTER MEMORIAL BRANCH LIBRARY
NEWTON COUNTY LIBRARY SYSTEM
6191 HIGHWAY 212
COVINGTON, GA 30016

LERNER PUBLICATIONS COMPANY · MINNEAPOLIS

The text of this book is printed on Lustro Offset Environmental paper, which is made with **30 percent recycled post-consumer waste fibers**. Using paper with post-consumer waste fibers helps to protect endangered forests, conserve mature trees, keep used paper out of landfills, save energy in the manufacturing process, and reduce greenhouse gas emissions. The remaining fiber comes from forestlands that are managed in a socially and environmentally responsible way, as certified by independent organizations. Also, the mills that manufactured this paper purchased certified renewable energy, such as solar or wind energy, to cover its production.

To people who care for the forests

Text copyright © 2009 by Valerie Rapp

All rights reserved. International copyright secured. No part of this book may be reproduced, stored in a retrieval system, or transmitted in any form or by any means—electronic, mechanical, photocopying, recording, or otherwise—without the prior written permission of Lerner Publishing Group, Inc., except for the inclusion of brief quotations in an acknowledged review.

Lerner Publications Company
A division of Lerner Publishing Group, Inc.
241 First Avenue North
Minneapolis, MN 55401 U.S.A.

Website address: www.lernerbooks.com

Library of Congress Cataloging-in-Publication Data

Rapp, Valerie.
    Protecting Earth's land / by Valerie Rapp.
        p.   cm. — (Saving our living Earth)
    Includes bibliographical references and index.
    ISBN 978-0-8225-7559-7 (lib. bdg. : alk. paper)
    1. Environmental sciences. 2. Environmentalism. 3. Green movement. I. Title.
GE105.R37 2009
333.72–dc22   2008003549

Manufactured in the United States of America
1 2 3 4 5 6 — DP — 14 13 12 11 10 09

CONTENTS

INTRODUCTION

Land is the solid ground beneath our feet. We know that plants need the land to live. Sometimes it's hard to understand how much we depend on the land too. We don't actually have roots in the soil like plants do. But like all plants and animals, we depend on the land for food, shelter, and safety.

Wherever you call home, all 6.6 billion of us live on the 30 percent of Earth's surface that is land. All the rest is covered by water. Although we swim, humans are land animals.

People can't live without land and its resources. We need forests for our wood and the paper and cardboard made from it. Rivers and lakes supply us

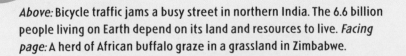

Above: Bicycle traffic jams a busy street in northern India. The 6.6 billion people living on Earth depend on its land and resources to live. *Facing page:* A herd of African buffalo graze in a grassland in Zimbabwe.

with water. We depend on farmlands for our food and for the cotton and wool that are used to make clothes. The food we eat comes from plants that grew in the soil or from animals that ate those plants.

We have many names for land—forests, deserts, and grasslands are just a few. These are all names of ecosystems. An ecosystem includes all the living things and the nonliving things, such as soil, water, and weather, of one place. Earth's many land areas have thousands of different ecosystems. Ecosystems include people too!

Healthy ecosystems include a wide variety of plants and animals. All the variety of plants, animals, and ecosystems around the world is called biodiversity. We can think of all these ecosystems as the web of life. The web of life is strong because it has many strands. If one strand tears, other strands hold the web together. If too many strands are torn, the web is weakened.

When ecosystems are damaged, people, plants, and animals are often hurt too. All living things benefit when the web of life is strong and healthy.

5

OUR ROOTS IN THE LAND

Do you live where it snows in the winter? Do you live where it hardly ever rains or where it rains often? Differences in weather patterns, or climate, lead to different ecological communities. The world's main types of ecological communities are called biomes. Tropical forests, deserts, and grasslands are some of the world's biomes.

The world's hottest weather is found in the tropical regions around Earth's wide middle, on both sides of the equator. The equator is the imaginary line halfway between the North Pole and South Pole. Tropical lands can be wet, like jungles, or dry, like the Sahara. Polar regions, the lands around the North Pole and South Pole, are Earth's coldest places. The ground is frozen most of the year and often covered by snow and ice. In between the hot tropics and the cold polar regions are Earth's two temperate zones. These in-between zones have four seasons—spring, summer, fall, and winter.

Earth is carved into mountains, valleys, hills, and many other landforms These landforms affect the climate too. When storm clouds hit a mountain range, the clouds drop much of their water, almost like water balloons hitting a wall. Because most of the rain falls on one side of a mountain range, the land on the other side is usually drier. Snow and rain that fall in the

People have adopted ways of life that help them survive in the places they call home. *Facing page:* In the Arctic near the North Pole, people have to protect themselves from the cold in the winter. *Below:* People keep cool in the hot tropics with open houses that let heat escape. *Background image:* Houses in a village in the Austrian Alps cling to steep mountainsides.

BIOMES AND LANDFORMS

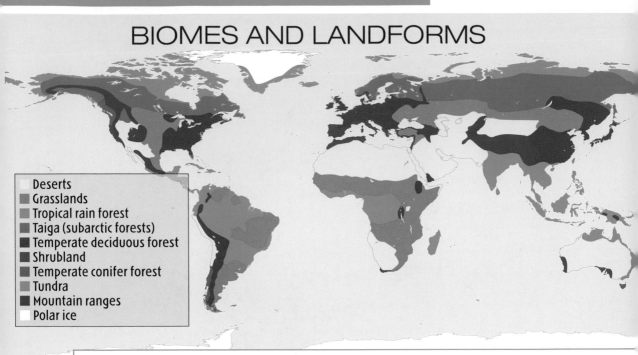

Deserts
Grasslands
Tropical rain forest
Taiga (subarctic forests)
Temperate deciduous forest
Shrubland
Temperate conifer forest
Tundra
Mountain ranges
Polar ice

This map shows the world's various biomes. It also notes mountain ranges and polar ice. These landforms can affect climate. Climate influences where biomes appear.

8

mountains are the source of the world's great rivers. Only about one-fifth of the world's people live in or near mountains. But more than half the world's people depend on freshwater that comes from mountains.

Climate makes a big difference in what kinds of plants and animals are found in an ecosystem. Every species of plant or animal has a natural habitat, or a place in nature where it normally lives.

Forests develop where enough rain falls for trees to grow. In northern Canada, hardy birch and spruce trees survive long, cold winters. In the hot tropics, hundreds of tree species grow in jungles. Many forests in the western United States have mostly conifer trees such as pines, which have needles instead of leaves. Hardwood trees such as oaks and maples lose their leaves each fall. They grow new leaves each spring.

Almost half of Earth's land area is deserts and dry grasslands. Little rain falls and few plants grow in these drylands. Drylands can be hot or cold. Deserts get less than 10 inches (25 centimeters) of rain each year. Dry grasslands get between 10 and 20 inches (25 and 50 cm) of rain each year. This is enough for wild grasses and scattered shrubs to grow, but not enough for forests. About one-third of the world's people live in some form of dryland.

People raise farm crops on about one-quarter of Earth's land area. Farms can be on land that used to be forests or grasslands, as long as the land has good soil. Even drylands can support farms, as farmers often bring water from distant rivers or lakes for their crops.

Farmers in Shropshire in western England divide the land into fields for growing crops. Farmland has replaced much of the native forests in regions around the world.

More than eight million people live in New York City, making it one of the most populated cities in the world.

Cities only take up a small part of the world's land. But about half the people in the world live in cities. A city is like a hub or a center for the land surrounding it. Steady streams of people in trucks, cars, trains, and airplanes move in and out of cities all the time, usually from all directions. People in cities need food, water, electricity, gasoline, and othe goods. Most of these resources are brought or created from lands outside the city.

THE STUFF LAND IS MADE OF

Soil is dirty stuff! But that's what land is made of. Life on land depends on the soil. Knowing about soil will help you understand the challenges we face in protecting and preserving our land. Let's see what soil really is, how it forms, and why it's so valuable to us.

The bits of dirt that crumble in your hand when you pick up soil are made partly from tiny grains of rocks. Water and wind wear down even the biggest rocks over time. Water carries rock minerals downhill, and wind carries rock dust to new ground. Minerals in the rocks join the soil and become nutrients. These nutrients help living things grow.

Soil is also made up of organic matter. Organic matter comes from anything that was once alive. Sticks, leaves, dead insects, rotten apples, and animal droppings are all organic. Once these things fall to the ground, they decay, or break down, and become part of the soil.

Air and water fill the spaces between particles of rocks and organic matter. Soil is the entire mixture of rock particles, bits of organic matter, air, and water. Plants grow best in topsoil, the soil on the surface. Topsoil is usually richest in nutrients.

Plants take in the soil's nutrients through their roots. The nutrients in soil are like

HOW MOUNTAINS ARE CARRIED TO THE SEA

Have you seen rain cut little trails into a hillside or road bank? Have you ever seen a river turn brown after a hard rain? Then you've seen erosion. The brown color comes from dirt washed into the river by the rain.

Sometimes whole mountainsides crash down in landslides, but most of the time, erosion happens slowly. Raindrops cut away grains of rock, an action called weathering. Ice cracks rocks and breaks off splinters. Flowing water carries rocks and soil downhill. Over millions of years, water carries an entire mountain to the sea—one little piece at a time.

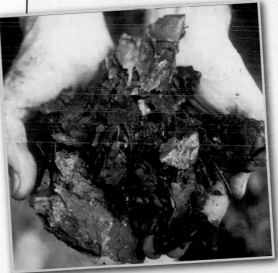

Leaves and other organic matter decay and return to the soil to supply nutrients for plant growth.

Good topsoil feels like damp breadcrumbs when you squeeze a handful.

EASY TO LOSE

It takes five hundred years or more for nature to create 1 inch (2.5 cm) of topsoil. It takes that long to wear rocks down into tiny grains and for organic matter to build a rich mix of nutrients into the soil. But that inch of topsoil can be lost in one heavy rainstorm. In the twentieth century, it took just forty years for one-third of the topsoil in the United States to erode and wash away.

food in the cupboard for plants. Nature constantly refills the cupboard by recycling nutrients from dead plants and animals back into the soil. Nature's cleanup crews are fungus, insects, mites (tiny spiderlike animals), and bacteria (tiny life-forms). Earthworms, bacteria, and other tiny living things in the soil chew up and digest dead plants. They turn all those fallen leaves and brown stems back into minerals in the soil. Plants pull the minerals up through their roots.

When a tree falls in the forest, fungus, mold, ants, beetles, and dozens of other species begin to take it apart. They soften, shred, tunnel through, and even eat the wood, breaking the fallen tree down into nutrients. Eventually, tree seeds sprout in the rotten wood and use the recycled nutrients to grow into new trees.

A fallen tree in this forest in Sweden gets turned back into soil with the help of fungus, mold, and insects.

When we eat plants—and meat from animals that ate plants—we get the nutrients from soil into our bodies. If the minerals aren't in the soil for the plants to absorb, then we don't get the minerals we need in our diet. So we depend on rich, fertile soil to grow food that keeps us healthy.

GIVING BACK TO THE SOIL

When it rains, much of the water soaks into the ground. Soil stores the rainwater for a long time after the rain stops. Trees and other plants, like all living things, need water to survive. They find their water in the soil, pulling it up through their roots. Water underground moves slowly through the soil, in time reaching rivers. Because the ground only lets go of water slowly, rivers have water all the time, even when it doesn't rain.

Plants don't just take minerals and water from the soil. Plants also give back to the soil. Growing roots push through the tiny spaces in soil and form an

Plant roots take water and nutrients from the soil. Root systems also help keep topsoil in place.

underground web that holds the soil together. Have you ever pulled a weed out of a flower bed? Soil clings to the plant's roots in a big clump. Shake the weed hard! Some dirt falls off, but not all of it. Grass, flowers, and trees grow a thick tangle of roots that secure the soil in place. Without the roots, the soil might erode (be blown or washed away) by wind or water.

Trees use lots of water, but trees also help the soil store water. Trees shade the ground, keeping it cooler on hot days. You feel this natural air-conditioning every time you sit in the shade under a tree. In hot, dry weather, soil in the shade doesn't dry out as fast. During a long dry spell, grass and flowers in the shade—where soil is moist—have a better chance of surviving. Forests keep an entire area cooler in hot weather.

THE SKIN OF EARTH

Soil is a thin layer on Earth's surface. Canadian scientist David Suzuki uses a comparison that shows just how thin this all-important layer of soil is. He asks students to picture a giant tomato 230 feet (70 meters) across. It has paper-thin skin just like a regular tomato. That's how thin the layer of soil is on our planet Earth. We depend on that thin layer for our food.

14

THE SHELTER OF TREES

Forests do much more for us than just offer shade and quiet, beautiful places to walk. Forests protect our water supply and help make rain. They even help our air.

Forest soils help filter water and keep it clean and pure. Many large cities around the world depend on water that comes from distant forests for their drinking water. In fact, 4.6 billion people—more than two-thirds of the world population—depend on forests for some or all of their water.

Trees recycle the rain. When rain falls, tree roots absorb water. Trees pull water from the soil up into their trunks, all the way up to their leaves. Forests hold huge amounts of water, just like big, thick sponges.

Mountain bikers enjoy a ride on a shade-covered trail in Monongahela National Forest in West Virginia.

Tree leaves use some water as they grow. But they let much of it escape into the air as water vapor. The water is recycled to fall again as rain on the same forest. Or wind may carry the moisture farther inland where it rains on other land. Forests recycle water again and again, losing only a little bit each time.

When forests are lost, trees no longer shade the ground or draw water from the soil. Rainwater runs off quickly and can flood fields and forests downstream. The water is gone so fast that it isn't recycled within the forest or inland. So when forests are lost, the first result is floods. The next result is less rain.

Forests help to clean the air too. Like all plants, trees take in carbon dioxide, a gas that is in the air. They also take in sunlight and pull up water through their roots. Using energy from sunlight, they turn the carbon dioxide and water into food. This process, called photosynthesis, releases oxygen back into the air. As trees and plants grow, they produce the oxygen that people and animals

16

Loggers clear trees in this forest in Massachusetts. If young trees are planted soon, a new forest can grow and protect the soil.

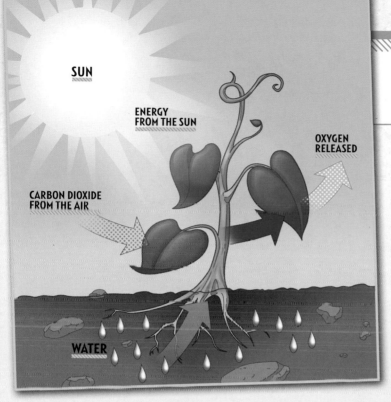

SUN

ENERGY FROM THE SUN

OXYGEN RELEASED

CARBON DIOXIDE FROM THE AIR

WATER

During photosynthesis, plants take carbon dioxide from the air and release oxygen.

breathe in. Just two healthy trees make enough oxygen to meet one person's needs on a daily basis.

Carbon dioxide occurs naturally, but since the 1800s, the level of carbon dioxide in the air has been slowly rising worldwide. Scientists believe the higher level of carbon dioxide is leading to global warming, the slow warming of Earth's climate. Trees can absorb carbon dioxide, storing it as carbon. In this way, trees help keep the gases in our atmosphere in balance. When a tree dies, the process of decay changes the carbon back into the gas, and it is released into the air as carbon dioxide.

THE LAND COMMUNITY

All around the globe, in every ecosystem, life on land depends on the soil. Rich, healthy soil produces the food we eat. Plants and trees protect the soil. Land is really a community that includes all the plants and animals that live on it. To take care of the land, we need to understand how the land community works.

CHAPTER TWO

LIFE IN A CROWDED WORLD

Earth is becoming more crowded every day. In just the fifty-eight years from 1950 to 2008, the world population grew from 2.5 billion to 6.6 billion people. The population has grown the fastest in some countries of Asia and Africa. The two countries with the most people are in Asia. China has 1.3 billion people, and India has 1.1 billion people.

It takes a lot of food to feed billions of people around the world. All those people also need places to live, energy to cook food and heat their homes, and clothes to wear. Those are just people's basic needs. We all enjoy having the things that make life fun too—sports, books, computers, games, and music, for example.

We use the land to meet all these needs. But growing populations can place heavy demands on land's resources. Most changes humans have made to ecosystems have been to meet people's needs. These changes sometimes damage the land.

Growing populations place heavy demands on land's resources.

18

Because world population continues to grow, the total amount of food and energy needed to sustain it keeps growing too. *Facing page:* Crowds in China, the world's most populous country, walk through a street in Beijing. *This page:* Kolkata, India, has one of the highest population densities (people per square mile) in the world.

SHRINKING FORESTS

Earth has lost about half of the forests that it once had. In 2008 forests covered about 30 percent of Earth's land area—about 10 billion acres (4 billion hectares). That's only half as many forests as Earth had three hundred years ago.

FORESTS RETURN IN NEW ENGLAND

In the time of the pilgrims, stately forests of sugar maple, beech, oak, hickory, and other trees covered the hillsides of New England in the northeastern United States. In the 1700s and early 1800s, many of these hardwood forests were cleared for small farms. The thin, rocky soil on the steep hills eroded easily.

During the 1800s, farming moved to the flatlands and rich soils of the Midwest and Great Plains. Forests slowly returned to the New England hills. Almost three-fourths of the New England countryside is covered again with the hardwood forests famous for their brilliant colors in the fall.

The world's forests are shrinking as land is cleared for farms, homes, and towns for the world's growing population.

Forests are also logged because people need wood. Much of the world uses wood as fuel for cooking and heating. Logs are milled into boards and beams for houses, other buildings, and furniture. Wood is also shredded into tiny pieces and used to make all different kinds of paper, from books to birthday cards. To meet all these needs, more and more forests have been logged around the world.

Forests have not been lost evenly around the world. In North America, Europe, and some Asian countries such as China and Japan, forests are multiplying and covering more ground. These countries protect some forests from logging. They use tree plantations to supply wood. Tree plantations are areas where trees are planted, cared for, logged, and then planted again. Logging may take place anywhere from five to sixty years after the trees are planted.

China, Russia, and the United States are using tree plantations more and more to meet people's wood and paper needs. In fact, over one-third of the global wood supply comes from tree plantations. Plantations, where often all the trees are of one species and the same age, are not the same as wild forests. But they can supply the wood that people need, which helps to save wild forests.

In many other countries, however, the need for wood or the desire to clear land leads to logging without tree planting. In the twenty-first century, Africa is losing its forests the fastest, with most of these trees cut for fuel wood. Even in the cities, wood is the only fuel available to many African people. South America is losing its forests almost as fast as Africa, with forests steadily logged around the edges of the Amazon River basin.

Soybean farmers in Brazil cut down 6.4 million acres (2.6 million hectares) of rain forests in 2004, one of the worst years for amount of forest lost in the twenty-first century.

Forests are being lost in many other countries too, including Mexico, countries of Southeast Asia and in the South Pacific, and in parts of Siberia in northern Asia. These countries have not yet been able to control the amount of logging in their forests. And they do not yet require planting trees so that new forests grow where old ones are cut down.

When no trees are planted, rain washes away the soil. Few trees grow back on the eroded land. As forests disappear or are damaged, forest animals have less habitat. People have a hard time getting the wood they need.

On this land in Peru, trees were cut down and roads built so mining could start. Without trees, more soil is lost every time it rains.

These large cacti survive on very little water in the desert of Baja California, Mexico.

DESERTS AND DRYLANDS

Life in the world's deserts has learned many tricks for surviving on little water. In the American Southwest, the tough mesquite tree grows thick, long roots, called taproots. Taproots go down 100 feet (30 m) or more into the ground, searching out deep sources of water.

Farther south in Mexico's Baja California desert, cardon cacti grow as tall as trees. They store water in their spongy pulp and protect themselves with nasty thorns. The vertical ribs of a cactus's trunk shrink closer together when the cactus loses water.

24

Herders tend sheep in a dry region of northern Kazakhstan in central Asia. Trampling and grazing by livestock can damage the delicate ecosystem on which these people have come to depend.

Desert people know many ways to survive too. They have lived for thousands of years in the deserts and drylands that cover 41 percent of Earth's land surface. More than two billion people—and an even greater number of cattle, sheep, and goats—live in lands that get little rain.

Dryland ecosystems are easily damaged, though. When too many people try to survive in drylands, they can't help but damage the land. Once these fragile ecosystems are damaged, they are slow to heal. That makes it even harder for people to make a living there. In many countries, families who live in drylands are the poorest families and have the most health problems.

EXPANDING DESERTS

The meager grasses and shrubs of drylands are all the lands have to protect their thin soil. If sheep and goats eat the grass down to stubble, the grass dies. If the shrubs are cut or the ground is cleared, the light desert soils are open to the wind. The sharp hooves of livestock or the rubber tires of off-road vehicles can pound desert soils into dust. Wind blows the dry, bare soil away, and the desert spreads.

Most of this loss of soil is caused by human activity, and erosion is the main way that people are damaging soil. Dust bowls are created when the plant cover is lost. Dry soils crumble into dust picked up by the wind. In the United States in the 1930s, parts of the prairies turned into a dust bowl. Lands too dry for farming were plowed and then a drought struck. Hundreds of thousands of people left behind failed farms and empty farmhouses. Entire families moved to other states.

A huge dust cloud blows through a New Mexico town in 1937. A severe drought combined with poor farming practices led to the Dust Bowl.

25

U.S. farmers changed the way they farm, preventing another dust bowl in the Great Plains. But the same pattern is happening in many places around the world. Overgrazing or poor farming practices are damaging many drylands. As a result, topsoil is being lost.

In the last fifty years, farmers plowed new wheat fields in northern and western China, a region near Mongolia. They planned to help feed China's growing population. But right away, the wind began to erode the soil of this newly plowed land. After just a few years, farmers are abandoning these new fields.

Thousands of villages are also being abandoned. Huge dust storms carry away millions of tons of topsoil from China. The dust storms blow eastward all the way across the Pacific Ocean, reaching the western United States.

On this map, red spots show where forests were lost from 1980 to 2000. Dark green shows where forests were gained in those same years. The olive green shows where soil eroded on drylands in the last fifty years.

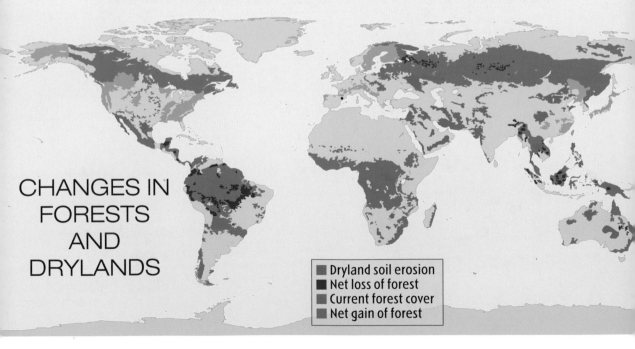

CHANGES IN
FORESTS
AND
DRYLANDS

- Dryland soil erosion
- Net loss of forest
- Current forest cover
- Net gain of forest

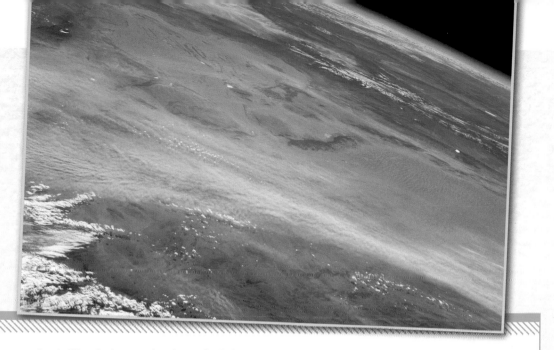

A satellite photo reveals a large dust storm moving across China from the Gobi Desert. The light brown color in the photo is fine sand blown by the wind.

As forests and soil disappear, deserts advance in long fingers. Around the world, almost half of all grasslands have some damage. The damage is easily seen in the drylands of the Middle East and central Asia. In Iran and Afghanistan, many villages have been abandoned because desert sands are burying buildings and roads. Desert lands are spreading in Africa as well. The dunes of the Sahara are advancing on Nouakchott, the capital city of Mauritania, a country in northwestern Africa. With the Atlantic Ocean to the west, the families of Nouakchott have nowhere to retreat from the ocean of sand moving toward them.

GIANT DUST STORM CROSSES OCEAN

Africa loses 2 to 3 billion tons (1.8 to 2.7 billion metric tons) of soil annually in dust storms. One giant dust storm out of central Africa was 3,300 miles (5,300 kilometers) across. The wind blew it west, all the way across the Atlantic Ocean to the Caribbean Sea.

LOSS OF BIODIVERSITY

As more forests disappear, soils erode, and deserts expand, many habitats are lost. In coming years, damage to the world's lands will threaten much of nature's biodiversity. Many wild animals are losing ground. These species are becoming endangered. In other words, they are in danger of becoming extinct, dying out completely. Extinction means that no more animals of that species will ever be born.

Extinction happens for many reasons. But human activities are pushing many wild animal species—and plant species too—toward extinction. Scientists estimate that almost one-third of mammal, bird, and amphibian species on Earth are facing the threat of extinction in the next century.

Extinction means that no more animals of that species will ever be born.

28

WILDLIFE ON THE MOVE

Earth is home to more people every year, leaving fewer wild places. As habitats are lost, plants and animals either die out or look for new places to live.

Wild species have always traveled in search of food or to escape bad weather. Many birds fly south to warmer lands for the winter. In Africa large herds of zebras and wildebeest migrate to find water and grass in the dry season. This slow, natural movement of species is a normal part of healthy ecosystems.

But the loss of habitats has sent many wild species on the move to new homes. Some of these species blend easily into habitats where people live. The coyote

Coyotes are known for being clever and finding ways to survive in new habitats. This coyote was spotted running across Central Park in the center of New York City in 2006.

has spread from the American West, where it always lived, through much of North America. Coyotes have been found living in Central Park, right in the center of New York City. In 2005 a coyote managed to get into a Chicago deli at night. The next morning, the deli owner found the coyote eating sliced meats!

In modern times, people travel by plane, car, and ship faster than they've ever traveled before. And some wild species hitch rides to places they never would have reached on their own. Some of these hitchhiking species behave themselves, but others don't. They invade the new habitat. These invasive species can be plants, animals, or diseases. Invasive species can be pushy, displacing native plants and animals. Or invasive species may infect native species. For example, sudden oak death, an invasive fungus, is killing oak trees in California.

In the American West, the sagebrush ecosystem covers millions of acres. The greater sage grouse is a species of bird found only in sagebrush ecosystems. Cheatgrass is a major threat to this ecosystem. An invasive species, cheatgrass forces out native grasses but then dies quickly, cheating cattle and deer out of summer grazing. It fuels hot grass fires, which burn sagebrush. Cheatgrass then reseeds itself after the fires. Because of the cheatgrass and other stresses, the sagebrush ecosystem is in poor health across much of the American West. The greater sage grouse is at risk as its habitat changes.

30

NOT JUST SOIL

As we can see in the example of cheatgrass, changes in one part of an ecosystem affect the whole. Many changes are normal, and healthy land can adjust to these changes. But people's growing demands and invasive species can change land more than it can handle.

NEW ORLEANS AND THE HURRICANE

New Orleans

Wetlands are another important environment that is disappearing as people move in to build homes or farms on these lands. Wetlands are low-lying areas that have spongy or damp, muddy ground. They can help absorb and filter surface water. In freshwater wetlands, the soil is very rich and trees and plants thrive. Many migrating birds and other animals prefer wetlands.

Along the Gulf Coast of the southern United States, swamps, wetlands, and islands used to buffer New Orleans from hurricanes. But since the 1930s, people have destroyed at least 1.2 million acres (492,000 hectares) of wetlands along the Gulf Coast.

Few wetlands were left to protect New Orleans in 2005, when Hurricane Katrina blew in with winds of over 140 miles (225 km) per hour. The hurricane killed at least 1,300 people and destroyed much of the city.

American forester Aldo Leopold wrote in his 1949 book, *A Sand County Almanac*, "Land is not merely soil . . . it is a fountain of energy flowing through a circuit of soils, plants, and animals."

Aldo Leopold knew from his work with forests and wildlife that energy always keeps moving through healthy land. Energy moves up through the food chain—an earthworm is eaten by a robin, which is eaten by a red-tailed hawk. Energy goes from one place to another. A deer eats spring flowers and uses that energy to run through the woods. Most important, energy circles around. When a tree falls or a deer dies, decay returns their nutrients to the soil, where seedlings and next year's flowers take root.

We've seen some of the ways that soil, our forests and grasslands, and the land's biodiversity have been damaged. In the next chapters, we'll learn how people are fixing damage already done and finding creative ways to take care of the land.

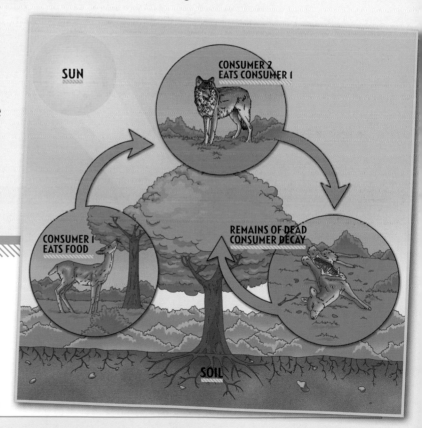

SUN

CONSUMER 2 EATS CONSUMER 1

CONSUMER 1 EATS FOOD

REMAINS OF DEAD CONSUMER DECAY

SOIL

This simple diagram shows how energy keeps moving in healthy ecosystems. Biodiversity creates many paths for energy to travel. With lots of pathways, healthy land is better able to handle floods, fires, and other events.

CHAPTER THREE

SAVING THE LAND: A LONG JOURNEY

Many ancient cities failed to survive to modern times. Their forests and topsoil were lost from careless use. Their rivers dried up, and their fields turned to dust. Wind blew sand against empty stone houses where once children played.

But other ancient societies saved their land. Six hundred years ago in the island-country of Iceland, farmers saw they had too many sheep on their highland pastures. The thin soil was being lost. They agreed among themselves that each farmer would keep fewer sheep—and they saved their pastures. The Iceland farmers still graze sheep on these pastures.

Over three hundred years ago in Japan, the shoguns, or leaders, ruled that logging would be strictly controlled. A few years later, they made rules about planting trees. Japan's beautiful forests still remain.

We too can take care of the land. In countries all around the world, people are protecting the soil, planting trees, and protecting wild areas.

We can do many things that help damaged land recover.

32

A deer walks through a forest of maple trees in Japan *(facing page)*, and sheep graze on grass in Iceland *(below)*. Hundreds of years ago, leaders in these countries made decisions that have helped protect land for future generations.

LAWS FOR THE LAND

Many countries of the world have passed laws to protect the land and our environment. The United States was the first country in the world to create a national park. In 1872 the U.S. government made Yellowstone National Park, high in the Rocky Mountains, protected land. It's protected for its natural beauty, rare geysers and hot springs, wildlife, and ecosystems.

The idea of national parks caught on around the world. More than one hundred thousand protected areas have been established worldwide. These areas represent about 12 percent of Earth's land. Protected places exist everywhere from Alaska's far north to tropical jungles to the very southern tip of South America. Countries generally give their highest level of protection to the places most important for their biodiversity or natural beauty.

Yellowstone National Park was named protected land in part because of its one-of-a-kind geysers, such as Castle Geyser *(below)*. Many years later, people began to value the biodiversity that is also protected in the park.

In the 1960s and 1970s, the United States passed new laws to protect the environment. The U.S. Endangered Species Act, passed in 1973, gives special protection to plant and animal species that are in danger of extinction in the United States. Many other countries have similar laws to protect species in trouble.

The United Nations is a group that works to solve problems affecting all countries. It leads the international fight to protect the environment. Through the United Nations, countries are talking about how to protect soil, stop habitat loss, and save endangered species. Countries are signing agreements, known as conventions, on what they will do. These agreements are just the beginning of a long journey toward success.

Many species of birds and land animals migrate across several countries. The UN Convention on Migratory Species helps to protect these migrating birds and animals. First signed in Iran, the UN Convention on Wetlands has led to the

PROTECTING ONE SMALL BIRD

The small aquatic warbler *(above)* nests in the marshes of Eastern Europe. In 2007 scientists discovered that the endangered warblers spent the winter in the wetlands of Djoudj National Park, Senegal, in western Africa. Senegal and Eastern European countries have all signed the UN treaties to protect wetlands and migratory birds. These countries are working together to protect both the summer and winter habitats of the aquatic warbler.

Members of the UN Convention to Combat Desertification hold a press conference for journalists.

protection of over 370 million acres (149.7 million hectares) in 154 countries. The convention named these areas as wetlands of international importance.

Expanding deserts don't respect the borders of countries. So the United Nations created the UN Convention to Combat Desertification. This helps countries fight to prevent deserts from taking over villages and grazing lands.

The UN Convention on Biological Diversity recognizes that protecting biodiversity is important for all the world's people. The countries that signed the treaty agree that biodiversity is about more than protecting plants and animals. It is about all people's need for a healthy environment. Protecting biodiversity—all the strands in the web of the environment—is an essential step in meeting these needs.

PROTECTING THE SOIL

All life on land depends on the soil. To save wildlife and the rest of our planet, we have to protect our soil. Luckily, people have figured out some good ways to do this.

Good farming is the best way to save topsoil. Farmers are updating time-tested methods such as crop rotation to protect soils. With this method, farmers change the crop they plant in a field from year to year. The farmer might plant alfalfa one year. Alfalfa adds some nutrients to the soil. The next year, the farmer plants a different crop. In drylands new ways of bringing water to fields, such as drip irrigation, make the best use of every drop of water.

Some land that erodes easily should never be farmed at all. In 1985 the United States started the Conservation Reserve Program to reduce soil erosion. The government paid farmers to stop farming lands that erode easily. They were encouraged to turn those lands into pasture or to plant trees instead. About 35 million acres (14 million hectares) of fragile soils were retired from farming. In just twelve years,

A drip irrigation system waters grapevines in Napa Valley, California. Less water is lost through drip irrigation than through traditional spray methods.

the program cut U.S. soil erosion dramatically. The loss of topsoil went from 3.1 billion tons (2.8 billion metric tons) every year to 1.9 billion tons (1.7 billion metric tons) every year.

China and other countries are also paying farmers to protect their lands and save the soil. But developing countries may need help in encouraging their farmers to take on new methods of farming to protect their topsoil. Scientists and teachers can help farmers find ways to grow crops and take good care of their soil.

On grazing lands, ranchers can protect the grasses and other plants that hold the soil in place. Ranchers can move their animals from one area to another over the grazing season. This way, grasses have time to grow back. On some grasslands, having fewer sheep, goats, and cows may let the grasslands recover. In some of Earth's driest regions, grazing animals may need to be removed entirely.

Women sit on recently felled logs. Slash-and-burn techniques were used to clear this rain forest for crops on the island of Sumatra, Indonesia.

People get water from a well in Mauritania in 2007. As trees around the well grow bigger, they will protect this water source from desert sand.

HOLDING BACK THE DESERT

In Africa the growing Sahara is destroying people's traditional ways of life. The battle against the advancing sand dunes is part of the battle for a better life. In the African country of Mauritania, desert nomads (people who travel with their grazing animals) have lost most of their livestock. Sand dunes have taken over their grasslands.

One group of nomads formed the Tenadi Cooperative in 1975. With little money and a fierce will to survive, this group began to create a new way of life for itself. The Tenadi Cooperative has planted rows of a mesquitelike desert tree to block sandstorms. These green walls of trees block wind, catch dust, and stop the advance of the desert. The living walls protect soil from being blown away. Also, the Tenadi Cooperative has drilled wells and created a date palm oasis around the wells. The wells are protected by their windbreak of trees.

Many families who were once nomads have settled around the Tenadi oasis. There they can grow garden crops under the date palms and harvest the dates.

A man photographs China's Green Wall in Inner Mongolia. As the trees grow taller, they will stop the expanding Gobi Desert.

CHINA'S GREEN WALL

China is growing the world's longest Green Wall. This living wall of trees will someday be 2,800 miles (4,480 km) long, stretching from outer Beijing to Inner Mongolia. It will take crews seventy years to plant all the trees!

The Tenadi Cooperative won a prize from the United Nations in 2006 for their work. And they began teaching other nomads these new ways to survive in the desert.

CLEANING UP POLLUTED SOIL

Leaks or larger spills of toxic chemicals sometimes happen in our modern world. These chemicals are absorbed by the soil and may stay for many years. Along highways and parking lots, spills of gasoline and other fuels can ruin good soil. Where mining is done, heavy metals and acids can remain. Toxic chemicals can kill plants and, sometimes, animals. If not cleaned up, the toxic chemicals can get into streams and other waterways.

The best way to protect soil from toxic chemicals is to prevent spills. But when toxic chemicals do spill, scientists and engineers are finding ways to clean them from the soil.

Some methods clean the soil right where it is. Workers can pump water into the polluted soil and then suck the water back out. The pumped water flushes the toxic chemical from the ground. In some cases, one chemical can be pumped underground to break down a toxic chemical into harmless substances. With some toxic chemicals, people have to dig up all the polluted soil and take it to a place where it can be safely treated.

Workers scoop up soil contaminated with toxic chemicals on the banks of the Kalamazoo River in Michigan.

CAN MUSHROOMS SAVE THE WORLD?

One man, Paul Stamets, has found that mushrooms can clean up some toxic chemicals. Stamets and his family run Fungi Perfecti, a mushroom business in the state of Washington. Mushrooms are just the "fruits" of fungi. Fungi live mostly underground and look like a network of white threads in the soil. Those thin white threads, called mycelia, break down rotting leaves and other organic material.

Mycelia can also break down some toxic wastes into harmless carbon and other elements. In one experiment, Stamets's crew put the mycelia of oyster mushrooms into the ground where diesel oil had spilled. After eight weeks, the mycelia had cleaned up 95 percent of the diesel oil. Large oyster mushrooms had sprouted. Stamets thinks that mushroom strains can be developed to clean up specific toxic wastes.

Some of the newest ways to clean up polluted soil use help from other living things. Scientists have found unusual bacteria that can destroy toxic chemicals. In one test, these bacteria cleaned up polluted soil at a gold mine in Nevada.

RESTORING FORESTS

Healthy forests protect soil, wildlife, and water quality. Where forestlands have been lost, people can restore them. In the forty years from 1960 to 2000, South Korea reforested its mountains. Forests have come back in New England and other parts of North America. China is planting millions of trees to expand its forests. Environmental groups such as World Wildlife Fund are building programs that pay some countries to grow more forests.

42

Programs that reward good forestry are also growing. In 2007 more than 215 million acres (87 million hectares) in over eighty-two countries were part of the Forest Stewardship Council (FSC) program that rewards good forestry. These practices allow foresters to use trees while still keeping forests strong and healthy. Officials from the FSC visit these forests, called eco-forests, to make sure that logging is done carefully. They make sure that trees are planted after logging and that soil, water, and wildlife in the forest are protected. The FSC label on paper, notebooks, and wood tells buyers that the products come from eco-forests.

One of the simplest ways to preserve forests is to reduce the amount of wood we use. In developed countries, saving

This FSC logo lets consumers know that this paper product was made with wood from forests whose management has been approved by the Forest Stewardship Council.

HARRY POTTER STANDS UP FOR ECO-FORESTS

About 33 million pounds (15 million kilograms) of paper went into making the twelve million copies in the first printing of *Harry Potter and the Deathly Hallows.* The U.S. publisher Scholastic wanted to find an environmentally sound way to make the books. It worked with the nonprofit Rainforest Alliance's SmartWood program to ensure that 65 percent of the paper came from eco-forests.

forests means recycling more paper. The United States uses more paper than any other country. In 1980 the United States recycled only about 25 percent of the paper used. But by 2003, Americans were recycling 48 percent, or almost half, of the paper used. That's good progress. But if the United States could recycle over 70 percent of paper, as Germany does, millions more trees could be saved. As other countries recycle more paper, even more trees can be saved.

Worldwide, over half of the wood taken from forests is used for fuel. In many developing countries, wood is the only fuel people have to cook their food. For people living in sunny places, solar cookers can be another way to cook dinner. Solar cookers capture and reflect the sun's rays to generate heat for cooking. These simple tools can save trees and money. Solar Cookers International and other groups are helping people in Kenya and other countries build or buy solar cookers.

COOKING WITH THE SUN

Simple solar cookers can be made from cardboard and aluminum foil for only three to five dollars. Once the cooker is made, cooking with the sun is free! It takes about three hours for a one-pot meal to cook.

SAVING WILD PLACES

The world's wild places are important in many ways, even for people who live far away. China learned how valuable its forests are only after many forests were cut down.

In China dense forests grow on mountains at the edge of the Tibetan Plateau. The Yangtze, the third-longest river in the world, begins deep within these mountains. These steep, misty mountains are home to many unusual plants and animals, including the endangered giant panda. The giant pandas feed on bamboo trees in the mountain forests.

In the 1980s, China began to establish protected reserves for the giant panda. But loggers continued to cut down the forests where the giant pandas lived.

Logging in the wild forests of the Tibetan Plateau threatened the giant pandas that lived there. The loss of trees also led to dramatic flooding on the Yangtze River.

As the pandas lost their native forests, the gentle bears retreated farther back into the mountains.

Beyond the mountains, the Yangtze provided water for rice fields, fish farms, and drinking water. More than 400 million people depended on the Yangtze River basin. These people went about their daily lives far away from the giant pandas. But in time, the heavy logging would hurt these people too.

In 1998 heavy rains fell. With few forests to soak up water and hold the soil in place, great floods poured down the Yangtze River. Millions of people lost their homes and farms. After the floods, the Chinese government banned logging of natural forests. The fir, spruce, birch, and bamboo forests of the mountains could

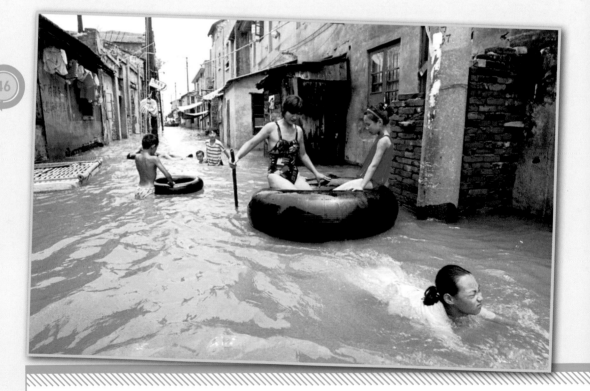

Families evacuated their homes in Wuhan, China, during the 1998 floods of the Yangtze.

Giant pandas eat bamboo in the Chengdu Panda Sanctuary and Rehabilitation Center—one of fifty protected areas the Chinese government has set aside to save the panda and its habitat.

no longer be cut. This decision helped all the people living downstream as well as the giant pandas and other wildlife.

China has fifty reserves protecting the giant pandas' forest habitat. Panda numbers are up to nearly sixteen hundred and continuing to rise. The Chinese government and international groups are helping local Chinese people near the reserves find jobs. The jobs are in sustainable forestry from tree plantations, tourism for reserve visitors, and reserve management.

Other countries have had tragedies similar to China's 1998 floods. With forests gone from the mountains, floods destroy people's homes and farms many miles downstream. Like China, other countries have acted to protect their forestlands. Countries that no longer allow any logging of their natural forests are New Zealand, the Philippines, Sri Lanka, Thailand, and Vietnam.

PROTECTING THE PROTECTED AREAS

Land is not always "saved" just by saying it is a protected area. The story of the wolves in Yellowstone National Park shows why all the species are needed for ecosystems to be healthy.

In the early 1900s, park rangers wanted to get rid of predators—animals like wolves that hunt other animals for food—in Yellowstone. Rangers and hunters killed all wolves in the park, and the herds of elk, deer, and bison grew. In a few years, many more elk and deer appeared. They ate all the young aspen shoots, nipped every new willow that sprouted, and grazed the wild grasses down to short stubble.

American forester Aldo Leopold saw that the elk herds were eating the park to death. He argued that wolves and other predators were needed in wild places. They keep the grazing animals trimmed to the number that the land can support.

It took many years for others to agree to this idea. Finally, in January 1995, wildlife biologists released fourteen wild Canadian wolves into Yellowstone National Park.

48

These were the park's first gray wolves in over sixty years. Rangers released another seventeen wolves into the park in 1996.

The gray wolves quickly took up hunting in their new home. Elk began to avoid places where

Government officials carry a gray wolf in Yellowstone National Park, where it will be released back into the wild.

wolves could catch them easily, such as thickets and steep stream banks. The park's first new aspens in years survived. Yellowstone's famous aspens began to grow back. Willow and cottonwood saplings sprouted near streams, and beavers returned to the park's streams. Wolves kept the number of coyotes down. With fewer coyotes, more pronghorn antelope fawns survived each spring.

RETURN OF THE WOLVES

At the end of 2006, just eleven years after wolves were returned to Yellowstone National Park, wildlife biologists found thirteen wolf packs in the park. Each pack has adult and pup wolves, and the thirteen packs had a total of 136 wolves.

The wolves' return to Yellowstone was a dramatic example of the value of biodiversity. Wildlife biologists call wolves a keystone species. If the keystone species is missing, the ecosystem changes in many ways. Without wolves, Yellowstone had too many elk and deer. As trees and shrubs were overgrazed, other wildlife species lost their habitats. Most scientists have come to agree that in wild areas, all native species should be protected.

49

With the wolves in Yellowstone keeping the number of coyotes down, more pronghorn antelope fawns survived each spring.

CHAPTER FOUR

FOOTPRINTS LEFT IN THE LAND

What can one person do to help protect the land? Denis Hayes was a student at Harvard when he organized Earth Day with the support of U.S. Senator Gaylord Nelson of Wisconsin and other leaders. The first Earth Day was celebrated across the United States on April 22, 1970. It helped launch the modern environmental movement, as people saw how many other men, women, and kids cared about the environment. All those people realized that together they could change the country.

50

And then people realized they could change the world! Earth Day is now celebrated every April 22 by more than 500 million people in 174 countries. Yet it began with one person and his idea. In this chapter, we'll look at what each of us can do to help protect the land.

Facing page top: Denis Hayes, the student who organized the first Earth Day, is shown on April 22, 1970, at the Environmental Teach-In headquarters in Washington, D.C. *Facing page bottom:* More than twenty thousand people gathered at a park in Philadelphia, Pennsylvania, to celebrate Earth Day in 1970. *This page:* Volunteers in Panama City, Panama, help clean up a beach on Earth Day in 2007.

THE GREEN BELT MOVEMENT

One woman in Kenya started a whole movement just by planting a few trees. In 1977 Wangari Maathai planted nine trees in her backyard. With those few trees, she planted the seeds of hope and started the Green Belt Movement. When Maathai was a girl, she played by a stream of clean, sparkling water. As the years went by, she saw that the stream dried up after forests were cut down. Village women then had to walk a long way to get water for their families. Maathai went on to get an education, which was very unusual for a country girl from Kenya. She was the first woman to be a professor at Kenya's University of Nairobi.

As a scientist, Wangari Maathai saw that villagers had hard lives because most of Kenya's forests had been lost. The farmers lost the food and firewood they used to get from the trees, and the soil was eroding. She saw also that the village women thought they were not smart enough to solve their own problems. They were waiting for others to help.

Then Maathai planted her nine trees and began a long journey to restore Kenya's forests and ease rural poverty. She encouraged other women to join her. Over the next thirty years, the women of the Green Belt Movement planted thirty million trees. These trees provide firewood, food, shade, and income for Kenyan farmers, and they protect the soil. Her journey also restored hope to Kenya's poor women, who began to believe that they were smart enough to solve problems. They learned that even though they were poor, they could restore their damaged land and improve their lives.

Wangari Maathai planted nine trees and began a long journey to restore Kenya's forests.

PLANTING TREES FOR PEACE

Peace trees have long been a tradition in Africa. To promote peace in Kenya, the Green Belt Movement inspired people to plant peace trees in villages and school yards. When Wangari Maathai won the Nobel Peace Prize in 2004 *(left)*, she asked schools around the world to plant a tree for peace on their school grounds.

Wangari Maathai became an important leader in Kenya's government. In 2004 she became the first African woman to win the Nobel Peace Prize. In her books and speeches, she tells the world that when we help Earth heal, we heal ourselves at the same time. Maathai has inspired people around the world to restore forests so their children can play by beautiful streams again. All this began with planting nine trees in a backyard.

LEARNING THE LAND

Saving the land and its ecosystems begins with learning about the natural world and how it works. People like forester Aldo Leopold and Wangari Maathai got to know the natural world as kids. Their love of nature inspired them to work for its good.

Nature scientists learn about Earth's lands and habitats by studying them up close. To find answers to their questions, they climb trees, snowshoe into the wilderness, and track wild animals. They also work in the lab, where they use microscopes and computers, along with other tools. But a modern scientist's most important tools

FOR THE BIRDS

Gabriela McCall Delgado *(below)* could identify ninety-five bird species of eastern Puerto Rico by the time she was sixteen years old. Using her own photos and working with biologists, she produced a sixty-page field guide to birds of Puerto Rico. She also developed a slide show and, for younger kids, a puzzle game about the birds. She speaks to school and community groups throughout Puerto Rico, inspiring them to protect bird habitats on this Caribbean island. In 2006 Gabriela received an International Young Eco-Hero Award for her work.

continue to be a sharp mind, a notebook, and a pen.

You can begin by learning about the land around you. How many of your local wild plants and animals do you know? Worldwatch Institute found that average Americans can recognize more than one thousand corporate logos, the colorful symbols of fast-food chains, brand-name shoes, and other companies. Those same average Americans recognize fewer than ten plant and animal species native to their area.

Can you learn the names of ten local, native species in the next year? Here's a tip: Ask your grandparents or other older people to help you. Also, check out field guides from your library.

MEASURING YOUR
ECOLOGICAL FOOTPRINT

Have you ever made footprints in the sand or the mud? When you look at the footprints,

you can see that a child's footprints are smaller than an adult's. When lots of people are on a beach, they cover the sand with footprints of all sizes.

Just as we can measure our footprint in the sand, we can measure our impact on the environment. The environmental group Earth Day Network came up with a way for each of us to see how our daily lives affect the environment. This measurement is called our ecological footprint.

Ecological footprints measure how many resources we use in our daily lives. One person's ecological footprint includes the land it takes to grow the food that person eats. It includes the land it takes to produce the wood, paper, cotton, and wool that person uses and the land needed to provide the energy that person uses. Finally, the footprint includes the land needed to hold the trash that person throws away. People who use more of nature's resources have bigger ecological footprints than people who use fewer resources.

HOW BIG IS YOUR FOOTPRINT?

You can find out your ecological footprint. Just take the Earth Day Network's simple quiz at www.myfootprint.org. The quiz asks where you live, how often you eat meat, how much garbage you throw away, and other simple questions.

55

Each of us can change our ecological footprints. Every time you walk somewhere instead of using a car, you save fuel and the resources that go into making it. This reduces your ecological footprint. Every time you recycle aluminum cans or newspapers, you cut back on the trash that goes into landfills. This also makes your ecological footprint smaller.

We can reduce our impact on the land by recycling more of the things we use. One of the best ways to recycle is also one of the easiest—dropping paper into recycling boxes. The more paper and cardboard that is recycled, the fewer trees that have to be cut down to make paper. Less logging helps save the world's shrinking forests.

Using recycled paper can also help. For instance, the average American uses about 730 pounds (331 kg) of paper each year. So an average three-person family uses a ton of paper each year. If that family uses all new paper, about twenty-four trees are cut down to make that ton of paper. If that family uses recycled paper for half of their paper needs, they can save twelve trees from being cut down.

Recycling newspaper is one way we can reduce the number of trees that are cut down to make paper.

GREEN SMARTS

Planting trees and gardening is a great way to get involved with regreening the land. In the city of Portland, Oregon, the historical Zenger Farm has been regreened as an urban farm. The 6-acre (2.4-hectare) farm and 10-acre (4-hectare) wetland are surrounded by warehouses, railroads, highways, and houses. But at Zenger Farm, people feel as if they've escaped the city. Kids get their hands dirty and grow sweet tomatoes, crunchy carrots, and other vegetables in the Grow Wise Youth Education Program at the farm. The farm even has a summer camp.

In Zenger's Immigrant Market Garden, the city's newcomers grow vegetables common in their home countries of the Middle East, Southeast Asia, Russia, and Mexico. Extra food from the farm is sold at local farmers' markets.

Kids at Zenger Farm prepare a delicious salad for their parents from vegetables they helped grow themselves.

FOOD FOR MONKEYS

Fourteen-year-old Winne Owade *(right)* helped regreen her home school and save a native animal. Wild monkeys were stealing food from farmers' fields near the Mbaga Girls' Boarding Primary School in Kenya. Winne learned that the monkeys were hungry because wild trees had been cut down. She got other students to help her collect leftover food from the school kitchen, which they put out where the monkeys could get it. Winne and the other girls are now helping to plant native fruit trees around the school so that the monkeys will have a wild food source again. The group Action for Nature awarded Winne an International Young Eco-Hero Award in 2005 for her leadership. She is the first African to get an Eco-Hero Award.

In cities around the world, creative people have turned backyards and vacant lots into gardens. City farmers in the African city of Accra, in Ghana, grow peppers, leafy greens, and onions for their families and for market. In Beijing, China, the city government encourages people to turn their rooftops into small gardens.

From forests to deserts, healthy ecosystems have some things in common. They have healthy soil and good biodiversity. Also, in healthy ecosystems, nutrients, or energy, keep moving from soil through plants and animals and back to the soil again. Every species plays a part. The Yellowstone ecosystem needs its wolves, elk, aspen, willows, beavers, and all the other species.

When trouble strikes—hurricanes, droughts, and fires—healthy ecosystems are tough enough to survive. Nature has many ways to rebuild ecosystems and bounce back from the damage. We can learn from nature how to help the land repair itself. But fixing the damage is slow, hard work. Taking good care of ecosystems in the first place is a smart idea.

Protecting land and biodiverse ecosystems takes care of people too. Natural forests prevent floods, tough trees stop the advance of deserts, and mushrooms clean up toxic wastes. We depend on the land for so much. If we take care of the land, it pays us back in many ways.

59

Protecting land
and biodiverse ecosystems
takes care of people too.

GOING GREEN

Young people are making a difference every day. In fact, lots of times kids are leading the way on making the world a greener, happier place—and adults are learning from them. Here are some ways you can help.

- **Reduce, reuse, and recycle!** The Earth Day Network calls these the "three golden R's of Earth care."

- **Keep old cell phones out of landfills.** The ReCellular Inc. website at http://www.recellular.com/recycling tells you how they help kids' groups raise money by recycling old cell phones locally.

- **Support eco-forests.** Ask your parents to buy school notebooks and paper that have a recycled paper symbol or FSC symbol. You'll know that fewer trees were cut down and young trees were planted after logging.

- **Explore the outdoors!** Check with your parents first, and always go with a buddy to be safe. You can learn about nature and have fun at the same time.

- **Learn the names of your local birds, trees, flowers, and animals.** Ask an adult or get a library book to help you learn the names. But never get close to wild animals and never feed them.

Exploring the outdoors is fun and helps us appreciate the land around our own homes.

- **Leave wild animals in their outdoor homes.** Wild animals are cute, but still wild. They may bite or scratch you. Adult animals may have babies depending on them for food, safely hidden in a nest or den. Baby animals have parents that are out getting food.

- **Visit nature parks with your family on weekends or vacations.** Your visits help to support these parks. Don't pick the wildflowers. And never litter!

- **Get involved with a local group to improve your local environment.** Plant trees, improve wildlife habitat, and do other fun stuff. See if you can get your whole family to join you!

61

GOING GREEN

Kids' ideas count too! You can tell your government leaders what you want them to do to protect the land. These leaders can pass laws to protect wild areas and endangered wildlife. They can decide to spend money on cleaning up toxic chemicals and damaged land. They also have the power to reward good farmers for taking care of the land.

Here are some tips on how to get started:

- **Tell them what you think about environmental problems.** Your letter doesn't have to be long. Explain why you think this is important, in your own words.

- **Explain exactly what you would like them to do.** For example, tell them if you think they should vote for or against programs to prevent soil erosion, protect forests, and help wildlife.

- **In the United States, you can find the names of all elected officials at one website: www.usa.gov.** Click on "Contact elected officials" to find the senators and congressional representatives for your state. You can send an e-mail to elected officials directly from the website!

Many environmental groups offer information about land and how you can protect it. On the next page are just a few:

62

- **Conservation International**
  http://www.conservation.org
  2011 Crystal Drive, Suite 500
  Arlington, VA 22202
  800-429-5660
- **Environmental Defense**
  http://www.environmentaldefense.org
  257 Park Avenue South
  New York, NY 10010
  800-684-3322
- **Natural Resources Defense Council**
  http://www.nrdc.org
  In Spanish: http://www.nrdc.org/laondaverde
  40 West 20th Street
  New York, NY 10011
  212-727-2700
- **The Nature Conservancy**
  http://nature.org
  4245 North Fairfax Drive, Suite 100
  Arlington, VA 22203-1606
  703-841-5300
- **WWF International**
  http://www.wwf.org
  Av. du Mont Blanc 1196
  Gland, Switzerland
  41 22 364 91 11

63

GLOSSARY

bacteria: tiny living things that are each made up of just one cell. Bacteria can only be seen under a microscope.

biodiverse: home to many different types of living things

biodiversity: the condition of nature in which many different types of living things inhabit the same area

biome: a major type of ecological community. Forests, deserts, and grasslands are types of biomes.

deciduous forest: a forest that grows in a temperate zone and whose trees have leaves that fall off in the winter

dryland: lands that get less than 20 inches (50 cm) of rain each year

ecological footprint: a measure of the amount of natural resources we use in our daily lives. The larger a person's ecological footprint is, the more impact that person has on Earth.

ecology: the scientific study of relations between living things and their environment

ecosystem: all the living things and the nonliving elements, such as soil, water, and weather of one area

endangered: in danger of going extinct. A species is endangered when the number of individuals drops so low that the species is close to disappearing.

erosion: wearing away by the movement of wind, water, or glaciers

extinct: gone forever. If a species is extinct, it means that no more individuals of that species can be born.

global warming: the warming of Earth because of increased carbon dioxide and other heat-trapping gases in the atmosphere. The theory of global warming has been supported by most scientific study.

habitat: the place in nature where a plant or animal normally lives

invasive species: a species that is not native to an ecosystem where it is found and that is also harming the ecosystem or making people sick

mycelium: a long, threadlike strand of a fungus that grows in the soil and that is the main part of the fungus. The plural of mycelium is mycelia.

organic: from or related to living things; any matter that is alive or was alive once and has the element of carbon

photosynthesis: the process by which plants use energy from the sun to convert carbon dioxide and water into sugar and oxygen

plantation: a large area that is farmed; often used to describe areas where trees are farmed

polar regions: the regions of Earth around the North Pole and the South Pole

species: kind

sustainable: practiced or used in a way that doesn't destroy or permanently damage a resource

temperate zones: the regions of Earth in the middle, between the polar regions and the tropics. The weather of temperate zones is in the middle too, not as cold as the polar regions and not as hot as the tropics.

tropics: the hottest regions of Earth, in a wide band that includes most of Africa, also Southeast Asia, Central America, and much of South America

SELECTED BIBLIOGRAPHY

Brown, Lester R. *Plan B 2.0: Rescuing a Planet under Stress and a Civilization in Trouble.* New York: W. W. Norton & Company, 2006.

Diamond, Jared. *Collapse: How Societies Choose to Fail or Succeed.* New York: Viking, 2005.

Global Footprint Network. "Ecological Footprint and Biocapacity Technical Notes: 2006 Edition." *Global Footprint Network.* 2006. http://www.footprintnetwork .org/2006technotes (June 5, 2008).

Holt, Kathleen, ed. "Land." Special issue, *Oregon Humanities.* Spring–Summer 2006.

Leopold, Aldo. *A Sand County Almanac and Sketches Here and There.* New York: Oxford University Press, 1949.

Loynachan, Thomas E., Kirk W. Brown, Terence H. Cooper, John M. Kimble, Murray H. Milford, and David B. Smith. *Soils, Society and the Environment.* Alexandria, VA: American Geological Institute, 2005.

Lomborg, Bjorn. *The Skeptical Environmentalist: Measuring the Real State of the World.* Cambridge: Cambridge University Press, 2006.

Millennium Ecosystem Assessment. *Ecosystems and Human Well-Being: Synthesis.* Washington, DC: Island Press, 2005.

Phillips, M. K., and D. W. Smith. *The Wolves of Yellowstone.* Stillwater, MN: Voyageur Press, 1996.

Suzuki, David, and Amanda McConnell. *The Sacred Balance: Rediscovering Our Place in Nature.* Vancouver: Greystone Books, 2002.

Trask, Crissy. *It's Easy Being Green: A Handbook for Earth-Friendly Living.* Salt Lake City: Gibbs Smith, Publisher, 2006.

Worldwatch Institute. *Vital Signs 2006–2007: The Trends That Are Shaping Our Future.* Washington, DC: Worldwatch Institute, 2006.

———. *2007 State of the World: Our Urban Future.* Washington, DC: Worldwatch Institute, 2007.

WWF-World Wide Fund for Nature (Formerly World Wildlife Fund). *Living Planet Report 2006.* April 11, 2007. http://www.panda.org/news_facts/publications/living_planet_report/lp_2006/index.cfm (June 5, 2008).

FURTHER READING

Can You Meet the Nature Challenge?
http://www.davidsuzuki.org/kids
Dr. David Suzuki, a Canadian scientist, has a website especially for kids. It includes the Nature Challenge for Kids (NC4K), homework help, games, activities, and puzzles about wildlife, nature, and the environment. Links lead to other fun science websites.

Celebrate Earth Day Year-Round
http://www.earthday.net
The Earth Day Network plans festivals and other events worldwide, not just on Earth Day but year-round. This site has great resources for kids and teachers. In one contest, schools that save the most energy can win prizes.

Dinerstein, Eric. *Tigerland and Other Unintended Destinations.* Washington, DC: Island Press, 2005. The chief scientist for WWF writes about his adventures with wildlife in wild places around the world. You'll also meet the amazing people who work to save these special places in nature.

Enter the EcoKids' Treehouse
http://www.ecokids.ca/pub/index.cfm
The EcoKids website is sponsored by Earth Day Canada. The lively website invites you to enter the EcoKids' Treehouse. You'll find lots of fun activities for kids. The site also has pages for teachers and parents.

The Green Belt Movement
: http://www.greenbeltmovement.org
The Green Belt Movement shares its know-how on its website. You can find more information about founder Wangari Maathai and the group's programs and activities.

World Wildlife Fund–International
: http://www.panda.org
The World Wildlife Fund–International website has loads of stories about how WWF is working with people in many countries to save endangered animals and places. The website offers homework help, virtual visits to WWF projects through Google Earth, and great photos of pandas, kangaroos, and other animals.

Shop Green
: http://www.ibuydifferent.org
The I Buy Different website has great ideas on how you can buy green every time you shop. It's sponsored by the WWF/Center for a New American Dream.

Stone, Lynn M. *Giant Pandas*. Minneapolis: Lerner Publications Company, 2004. This easy-to-read book with color photos describes the lives of giant pandas and the mountains where they live. It also explains why giant pandas are in danger and what people are doing to save them.

Suzuki, David, and Kathy Vanderlinden. *Eco-Fun: Great Projects, Experiments and Games for a Greener Earth*. Vancouver, BC: Greystone Books, 2001. This book has dozens of fun activities, using items you already have at home. Whether you break stones with a simple seed or grow a forest in a jar, you'll learn something about how the world works.

Suzuki, David, Kathy Vanderlinden, and Diane Swanson. *You Are the Earth: Know the Planet So You Can Make It Better.* Vancouver, BC: Greystone Books, 2003. This book uses science, fun facts, comics, and folktales to explain how people depend on Earth. The book covers air, water, soil, energy, and love. And it describes some things kids are doing for Earth.

Swinburne, Stephen. *Once a Wolf: How Wildlife Biologists Fought to Bring Back the Gray Wolf.* Boston: Houghton Mifflin, 2001. This book tells the story of the scientists bringing wolves back to Yellowstone. It also reviews the history of the gray wolf in the United States.

Take It Global!
http://www.takingitglobal.org
Young people around the world speak out in this online community. Kids can join the discussion boards about global and local issues, learn what other people are doing, and send in their own writing and art. The website has pages in ten other languages in addition to English.

What Animal Is That?
http://www.enature.com
The National Wildlife Federation's eNature site has online field guides where you can find out the names of animals and plants you see in the United States. You can save your own wildlife list on the site, use eCards to send nature images to friends, and take quizzes about your nature knowledge.

Where's the Science?
http://www.usgs.gov
Scientists from the U.S. Geological Survey have been studying Earth and nature for over 125 years. The website tells you what these scientists are learning about the life sciences and earth sciences in over one hundred countries.

INDEX

ABOUT THE AUTHOR

Valerie Rapp writes about how nature works, how people connect to nature, and how we're going to survive in the twenty-first century. She is the author of four books and many scientific publications. She and her husband have lived for many years in a log home in the Oregon mountains.

PHOTO ACKNOWLEDGMENTS

The images in this book are used with the permission of: © Photodisc/Getty Images, p. 1 (background, title), all page backgrounds; © iStockphoto.com/Nikolay Titov, pp. 1 (bottom left), 3 (top); AP Photo/Bullit Marquez, p. 3 (bottom); © Karen Kasmauski/Science Faction/Getty Images, p. 4 (inset); NASA/JSC, pp. 4-5; © Sergio Pitamitz/SuperStock, p. 5; © Scott Warren/Aurora/Getty Images, p. 6; © Karlene Schwartz, pp. 7, 12, 14 (top), 16; © Jeremy Horner/Riser/Getty Images, p. 7 (inset); © Bill Hauser/Independent Picture Service, pp. 8, 17, 26, 31; © Digital Vision/Getty Images, p. 9; © iStockphoto.com/Adam Kazmierski, p. 10; USDA Photo, p. 11; © Travel Ink/Gallo Images/Getty Images, p. 13; © iStockphoto.com/Klaudia Steiner, p. 14 (bottom); © Skip Brown/National Geographic/Getty Images, p. 15; AP Photo/Greg Baker, pp. 18, 46; © Hemis.fr/SuperStock, p. 19; © iStockphoto.com/Elena Elisseeva, p. 20; AP Photo/Alberto Cesar-Greenpeace/HO, p. 21; © Beth Wald/Aurora/Getty Images, p. 22; © Konrad Wothe/Minden Pictures/Getty Images, p. 23; © Igor Burgandinov/Art Directors, p. 24; AP Photo, pp. 25, 50 (both); Image Science and Analysis Laboratory, NASA Johnson Space Center, p. 27; AP Photo/Dima Gavrysh, p. 29; © iStockphoto.com/nicoolay, p. 30; © Steve Vidler/SuperStock, p. 32; © Bruno Morandi/Photographer's Choice/Getty Images, p. 33; © age fotostock/SuperStock, p. 34; © Martin Woike/Foto Natura/Minden Pictures/Getty Images, p. 35; UN Photo/Stephen Koh, p. 36; © Hendrik Holler/Bon Appetit/Alamy, p. 37; © David Clegg/Art Directors, p. 38; AP Photo/Schalk van Zuydam, p. 39; © Peter Parks/AFP/Getty Images, p. 40; © Jim West/ZUMA Press, p. 41; © iStockphoto.com/YinYang, p. 42; © Julie Caruso/Independent Picture Service, p. 43; © Chris de Bode/Panos Pictures, p. 44; © Keren Su/China Span/Alamy, p. 45; © Stuart Fox/Gallo Images/Getty Images, p. 47; National Park Service Photo by Jim Peaco, pp. 48, 49 (bottom); © iStockphoto.com/Denis Pepin, p. 49 (top); AP Photo/Arnulfo Franco, p. 51; AP Photo/Karel Prinsloo, p. 53; © Rick & Nora Bowers/Alamy, p. 54 (top); Courtesy of Action for Nature, www.actionfornature.org, pp. 54 (bottom), 58 (bottom); © Charles Gullung/Photonica/Getty Images, p. 55; © Russell Sadur/Dorling Kindersley/Getty Images, p. 56; © Peggy Acott/Portland Nursery, www.portlandnursery.com, p. 57; © iStockphoto.com/Graeme Purdy, p. 58 (top); © Peter Mason/Taxi/Getty Images, p. 61.

Frontcover: © Photodisc/Getty Images (background, title, spine); © David Young-Wolff/Photographer's Choice/Getty Images (left); © Karen Kasmauski/Science Faction/Getty Images (right); © iStockphoto.com/Nikolay Titov (bottom left). Back cover: © Photodisc/Getty Images.